REVELATIONS

Revelations
Copyright © 2018 by Ruben Quesada

Cover art: *Garden of Earthly Delights* by Hieronymus Bosch
(Public Domain)
Author photo by RS Jenkins
Cover design by Sibling Rivalry Press
Interior design by Bryan Borland

Sibling Rivalry Press, LLC
PO Box 26147
Little Rock, AR 72221
info@siblingrivalrypress.com
www.siblingrivalrypress.com

ISBN: 978-1-943977-54-3
First Sibling Rivalry Press Edition, November 2018

This title is housed in the Rare Book and Special
Collections Vault of the Library of Congress.

REVELATIONS

RUBEN QUESADA

SIBLING RIVALRY PRESS
LITTLE ROCK / ARKANSAS | DISTURB / ENRAPTURE

CONTENTS

ANGELS IN THE SUN

after Turner

I would have waited alone a thousand
years for the coming of angels,
blinding bright as the spring sun to arrive,

to abandon this world for another.
Stunned by their flashing lights aflame

across the bow of their space craft—landing

lights for that world. Herds of animals:
horses, humans, and fish fixed.
The angels approached.

Come angels! Come beasts!
Men and women cried out
to each other; the angels cried;

some were lost between their earthly life

and paradise and what is paradise, anyway?
Few imagined being bound to this world;

blue halo of emerald mountains;
extraordinary, ordinary—they rose,
a crucifixion yardarm flying away.

Porque nunca he querido dioses crucificados,
Tristes dioses que insultan
Esa tierra ardorosa que te hizo y te deshace.

Because I have never loved crucified gods,
Sad gods who insult
That ardent earth that made you and undoes you.

— Luis Cernuda

I

Christ was never more than a man nailed to a
cross but from him I learned that an entire life
fits into a person's palm like a book of poems
like an executioner's hammer now at thirty five
I have learned confession won't save me I'm
reminded of a fortune teller I met two years ago
in San Francisco at Dolores Park on a radiant
late afternoon as the sun slanted across bodies of
slackline-wrapped palm trees I too must have
been radiant having just listened to a poetry
reading by Guillermo Gómez-Peña in the Mission
from the shade came a woman in a green scarf
she pulled me toward her held my hand making
it float face up into the pool of air between us
her finger tracing my palm into creases of sevens
or ells she began to sketch a future I once wanted
a life of fortune and fame into neat curves from
thumb to wrist then my hand dropped her scarf
drifted into the trees she coughed the barrels of
her lungs exhausted she looked away wiping her
mouth and said last night it was quiet as your
mother died a haze of zinnias hushed in the rain

II

And an angel appeared and said come with me
to this place to bend and smell the stone roses
slowly budding below the window sill how it
lingers this sweet coral honeysuckle sap of earth
but what's best is on warm windy days when
the smell of Antilles lilies or petrichor washes
over me in a field like sea foam at my feet I lie
and close my eyes as donkeys pass in the caramel
sunlit marsh beyond the amplitude of my
outstretched knees in the marsh marigold glaze
I imagine a future where clouds fall from the
sky in the shape of seaside olive trees listen
children gaze into my eyes gaze into these honey
colored creatures listen to oxen file forward
into the horizon as each coarse head of the field
whips and pivots like the loose neck of a goose

III

This is how the dream begins I am standing on
our lawn and I watch her a girl in a black dress
waiting at the corner to cross the street my eyes
blur as tires and birds dart into trees then cars
begin to lose their slack and I see her body flail
my mother appears in a crowd of children they
stand tightly tucked up close to see the girl it is
Mary and there is my mother back from work
where she is part of an assembly line sorting letters
to places she'll never know Mary's face is as pale
as the color of skim milk her dress gone to asphalt
her eyes roll as she falls into my mother's arms
soon her mother will be found in their garage the
car running I am seven our class attends her funeral

IV

I wish it had only
been a dream after
thousands had died
finally then did
President Reagan say
AIDS then months
later an actor Rock
Hudson died there
was no funeral just a
body turned to ash

V

Lord if the ancient seahorses and whales
could flee they would surge into some
distant future light-years ahead like those
grey shadows waiting on a bough outside
my window on nights when I can't sleep I
see them they wait to abandon this world
they must be lost apostles not yet found by
scientists their space craft en route from a
remote half sleep region of space where the
sun has already abandoned its orbit it will
be discovered long after I am dead long
after wind shifts have broken the body of
this continent into pieces good Lord take
me where anything is possible goodbye
decaying mountain groves at the edge of
the world lord I am not afraid take me from
the worthless daemon of this daily life

VI

In 1987 I watch R Budd Dwyer give
his life away on broadcast television
he is surrounded by reporters they
are tired of his story how could this
be news I hear him say this will hurt
someone in an accent from the thick
skin of Missouri as cameras off screen
scream and startup he holds a revolver
the size of his head his hand is shaking
like the tail of a copperhead colt
slivering inside his body waiting to
rattle like the Holy Spirit out of his
head waiting to get out so it won't
come around to visit him again and
now every time I fall asleep I dream
it's me but instead of being a politician
I'm a teacher instead of being the
Treasurer of Pennsylvania I'm a poet

DESIRE

In the calm September field
from the yellow poplar
a leaf like a broken star
spins toward the earth

if this is the way of the soul
master of the stars and the leaves
transform a passionate shade
from life to death

By Luis Cernuda (1902 – 1963)
Translated from the original Spanish

VII

In this blood that haunts my skin in the
folds of my brain are burrowed the
harrowed words to describe you bleak
damned and when the universe was young
it possessed the means to give you breath
to deliver you to me here half alive
propped against the wall in the corner of
your room your straw colored hair padding
your chest knuckles and toes this was our
last day together you'd stumbled onto the
drawn curtain as we watched ghostly orbs
carry in the laughter of the neighbor's dog
outside children passed as an ice cream
truck's siren song shook you back to life
from the ghost of heroin photographs
browned like honey from years of smoke
covered the walls and I watched you from
your bed where so many worlds undressed
beneath the sap-like weight of phosphorous
oh bromine xenon oh astatine tellurium
what more could the periodic table offer
already you were nitrogen sulfur even gold

VIII

In early August my shirt is always wet from the heat
and summers simmer in silver patches of rain as I
board the outbound express my morning shift has
just ended through the glass the sun needles at my
neck as the car rails into a turn dives down into a
tunnel buried deep like the dead toward home where
no one will expect me I remember that afternoon
ten years ago when you returned from work and
found me gone I don't even know if you're still
alive and I don't care I remember that summer in
Dallas where we met I smoked a pack of Camel
cigarettes a day and drank iced tea by the pool staring
at the bald cypress trees that sagged around us one
day to surprise you I took the day off I did the
laundry found a syringe and tourniquet now as I
arrive at my stop the sun has gone at home the walls
keep time the clock dings it's half past eight the tree
tops begin to darken I sit at my desk take a rosary
of metal from the drawer I cradle the barrel like a
clarinet against my mouth the quick rhythm of the
second hand clicks and already the jacarandas have
started to push their tongues against the window

IX

Last night as we lay in bed we talked about one-night
stands we'd had you told me about the time in Salt
Lake City when you went away to college when you'd
spent a night in a sling high on heroin with a line of
married Mormon men waiting their turn to be inside
you the smell of the fireplace filling your nose is what
you remembered most beyond the window mountains
blanched with snow and this morning before you awoke
I kissed your half-open mouth I watched the blackening
snow bank along the curb as people slushed along the
sidewalk above us a hunk of clouds formed grackles
crackled above a church lot nothing more was said

WINTER SONG

As beautiful as fire
throbbing in the quiet western sky
       ardent golden

As beautiful as dreams
living inside the breast
       alone rescued

As beautiful as silence
vibrating around kisses
       alate sacred

By Luis Cernuda (1902 – 1963)
Translated from the original Spanish

X

I stand on the side of the road waiting
for rescue there was a time when youthful

sunsets were plum colored lights kissing snow
covered rooftops joy was a love letter
about the splintered edge of sentient
glaciers in Iceland melting into pale
green sea dreams of sleepy street lights

I am not alone an owl glides and its body billows
above into the pink anemone of dusk
into an open-mouthed window
where a skyline of high rises watch
cars ripple by like sequins stretched from coast

to coast everywhere every spring bloodied
cherry blossoms grow below back scattered
starlight I move toward approaching headlights
that conjure snowfall my nose burns somewhere

the thick arms of a pinyon pine smokes and as I call
out a dole of doves surges from my mouth like steam

XI

One morning the spirit of my lover's uncle returned
there was no fanfare no terror only a blue silhouette

translucent above our bed growing dim
I was the sole witness to this specter quiet

as the rising sun waking overhead I awakened
cold to see an Aegean blue figure hovering bedside

through his gaze and mustachioed grin
on the other side of his face a dazzling tremolo

of morning light streamed into this darkened space
and later that evening as we moved through

the neighborhood streets dead with aging trees
frozen sidewalks led us freely into the moonlight ahead

XII

As a boy I was unbearably uncomfortable
about my body and the men my mother dated
gave me erections in the bathroom
as I thought of them under the hiss
of the shower to drown out the cat calls
from boys at school who threatened to kill me

every afternoon and I have tried to avoid
blaming myself for being called a faggot
for most of my life I could not escape it
but those days have gone like the gospel
of Anita Bryant who wanted to drown

a faggot rebellion like that one at Stonewall
in the summer of 1969 and we shall overcome
once I was a man who curated mediocrity
like the time I misspelled peniaphobia
so as to conceal my fear of having spent my life
penniless undressing only in the dark

DEAD BIRD

Above the grey hillside
beneath new hawthorn leaves
at the foot of a gate where
squabs pass in red dress

your black and white wing torn
motionless in death   prickled
like a stem   a rose
a banished star from the throne of night

that broken body once captivated
the light the ardent song of dawn
at peace atop the coop of night

when love has gone   everything
seems useless   even heartbreak
suffering for beauty grows old
the eagerness of light drowns shadows

if only you were like the sea   born of its own
death   I see your shadow
sobbing for breath
that brief and alluring love affair with life

now silence   sleep   forget everything
death dwells in you it nourishes you
that wing's stillness   like a setting sun
it is better this way

By Luis Cernuda (1902 – 1963)
Translated from the original Spanish

XIII

Even the province of truth
must be stitched you must
start with a pattern in a bar
years ago a needle and thread

to sew the empty sleeves
of a sentence on a Saturday night
our history is predicated
upon subject and verb

a hole in the hull of a hemistich
we found a dark corner to name
the feeling that slowly sweeps
through the body it babbles

and burrows in the veins
as it charges the heart
the smell of our bronzed skin
in my mouth the silken road

of my spine against the wall
stitch the braided memory

of prepositions and interjections
remember to piece buttons

onto the cuff press an adverbial
crest over the breast and frenzied
fringe for flare your face in pink
neon no longer is a hanger

for shoulders to lean upon
a curled collar forms a question
finish with an explanation
what is your name

XIV

Beneath sunsets like wildfire
an alchemy of traffic in orange
and red on the 405 in Los Angeles

at the intersection of the 105 and the 110
is the tallest interchange ramp in the city
once shortly after the ramp opened for traffic

a man named Daniel V Jones drove to the top
after a car chase and there he parked it was late
in the afternoon after-school cartoons interrupted

to broadcast this man who would set himself on fire
he was already dying recently diagnosed with cancer
his HMO had failed to provide healthcare to save him

hair and clothes on fire he ran out of his truck
took a shot gun and shot himself in the head
the blown out windshield fluttered in the background

XV

dear sister remember that time

I was eight and I snuck a record
from your collection to listen to music

while streetlamp shadows shifted
on the snow vinyl spun in purple

like the sky shaping itself into inky streaks
as the hum of a ballad like a prayer

murmured throughout the house
now each morning I pray for silence

a pine in the backyard leans into the window
hoping to steal words to grip me in its drizzle

FALL FEELING

Upon the old ruins it rains,
　　　The autumn still green,
Odorless, dreams blossom,
　　　And the body gives in.

I'm raptured in the fountains,
　　　Along the valley there are sheer figures,
And amid the vast pale air, brilliant
　　　Blue wings.

Beyond the fresh babbling is the sacred
　　　Halo of death.
Nothing is gained nor lost.
　　　My memory grows dark.

Everything is true, except hate, as harsh
　　　As the grey clouds
Passing vainly above this treasure,
　　　Furiously made dim.

By Luis Cernuda (1902 – 1963)
Translated from the original Spanish

ACKNOWLEDGMENTS

"XI" appeared in *Poem-a-Day* from the Academy of American Poets on June 7, 2018, selected by D.A. Powell.

"Angels in the Sun" appears in *Best American Poetry 2018* selected by Dana Gioia.

Thank you to the editors of the following journals where these poems first appeared in some form:

American Poetry Review
Best American Poetry Blog
Boaat Press
Cimarron Review
Miramar
Ostrich Review
Pilgrimage
Rumpus Poetry
The Shallow Ends
Solo Novo
Southern Humanities Review
Spoon River Poetry Review
Stand
Taos Journal of Poetry & Art
TriQuarterly
Tupelo Quarterly

I am grateful to Ángel María Yanguas Cernuda for permission to publish translations of poetry by Luis Cernuda (1902 – 1963).

Thank you to the following institutions that gave me time, space, and often funding to write these poems over the years: CantoMundo, Napa Valley Writers' Conference, Red Lodge Clay Center, Eastern Illinois University.

Thanks to the following people who believed in me and offered their support over the years in some form: Jonathan Bohr Heinen, Brian Kornell, Rosebud Ben-Oni, Wesley Harvey, Don Share, D.A. Powell, Carmen Giménez Smith, Juan Felipe Herrera, Francisco Aragón, Deborah Paredes, Celeste Guzmán Mendoza, Dan Vera, Jeannie Ludlow, Michael Montlack, and Lisa Marie Basile.

Thank you to Spencer Reece and the Unamuno Author Series in Madrid for their vision and guidance on this project.

I am beholden to Seth Pennington and Bryan Borland of Sibling Rivalry Press for their time and care of this collection.

ABOUT THE POETS

Ruben Quesada is the author of *Next Extinct Mammal* and *Exiled from the Throne of Night: Selected Translations of Luis Cernuda*. He is currently editing a volume of essays by contemporary Latinx poets on poetry, *Latino Poetics* (University of New Mexico Press).

A gifted writer, editor, and translator with over a decade of practical experience and training, Quesada serves as faculty at Northwestern University, The School of the Art Institute, Vermont College of Fine Arts, Columbia College Chicago, and UCLA, where he teaches Latinx literatures, literary translation, editing, and poetry writing.

Luis Cernuda (1902 – 1963) was born in Seville, Spain. He was a member of Spain's influential group of poets, The Generation of '27. Remembered for his direct and colloquial language focused on intimacy and homosexuality, Cernuda wrote numerous collections of poetry. He was in exile from 1936 at the start of the Spanish Civil War and never returned. The selected translations in this chapbook are from his collection *Las nubes* (1937 – 40). The poems focus on his personal and spiritual crisis written at the start of his exile.

ABOUT THE PRESS

Sibling Rivalry Press is an independent press based in Little Rock, Arkansas. It is a sponsored project of Fractured Atlas, a nonprofit arts service organization. Contributions to support the operations of Sibling Rivalry Press are tax-deductible to the extent permitted by law. To contribute to the publication of more books like this one, please visit our website and click *donate*. We gratefully acknowledge the following donors, without whom this book would not be possible:

Liz Ahl

Stephanie Anderson

Priscilla Atkins

John Bateman

Sally Bellerose & Cynthia Suopis

Jen Benka

Dustin Brookshire

Sarah Browning

Russell Bunge

Michelle Castleberry

Don Cellini

Philip F. Clark

Risa Denenberg

Alex Gildzen

J. Andrew Goodman

Sara Gregory

Karen Hayes

Wayne B. Johnson & Marcos L. Martínez

Jessica Manack

Alicia Mountain

Rob Jacques

Nahal Suzanne Jamir

Bill La Civita

Mollie Lacy

Anthony Lioi

Catherine Lundoff

Adrian M.

Ed Madden

Open Mouth Reading Series

Red Hen Press

Steven Reigns

Paul Romero

Erik Schuckers

Alana Smoot

Stillhouse Press

KMA Sullivan

Billie Swift

Tony Taylor

Hugh Tipping

Eric Tran

Ursus Americanus Press

Julie Marie Wade

Ray Warman & Dan Kiser

Anonymous (14)